EXECUTION POEMS

EXECUTION POEMS

The Black Acadian Tragedy of
"George and Rue"

George Elliott Clarke

GASPEREAU PRESS MMI

For G.P-C, darling intellectual,
& Geraldine Elizabeth Clarke, beloved mother.

Per stygia, per manes vehor.
– Titus Andronicus

Beauty has the power to check aggression:
it forbids and immobilizes the aggressor.
– Marcuse

I alone of all things
Fret with unsluiced fire.
– Carman, Sappho, XLI

WHAT FOLLOWS IS THE TEXT of George Elliott Clarke's *Execution Poems*, a suite
of poems about his cousins, George and Rufus Hamilton, who were hanged
in July 1949 for the murder of a Fredericton, New Brunswick, taxi driver.

In early 2000, I contacted George Elliott Clarke to discuss the idea of
producing a small limited edition of his poetry the old-fashioned way – with
lead type and a hand press. As a printer and a designer, letterpress production
was new to me, and at that time had only printed a few cards and invitations
using this method. I was eager to embark on a more challenging project.
Clarke responded with *Execution Poems*.

What Clarke presents in *Execution Poems* is uncomfortable. He is remind-
ing us of racism and of poverty; of their brutal, tragic results. He is reminding
us of society's vengefulness. He is blurring the line between the perpetrator
and the victim – a line we'd prefer to be simple and clear. At the heart of it,
Clarke is frustrating the notion that society deals any better with these issues
today than it did in the 1940s. As all true poetry should, Clarke's embodies
both damnation and redemption, offering convoluted triumphs alongside
tragedy.

These poems were originally released in a hand-printed limited edition,
published by Gaspereau Press in December 2000. All 66 books in the edition
were sold within a month of its release. However, given the groundswell of
interest in *Execution Poems,* we decided that the poems would also be released
in this trade edition.

THE ORIGINAL EDITION of *Execution Poems* was produced as a folio, printed on
25 × 19 inch sheets which were folded once and trimmed to make a 12 × 18
inch book. The type used for this project was Monotype Bembo, hand com-
posed by Susan Baxter and Nyla Trimper. Producing a book with old type,
hand set from drawers, posed many challenges – damaged and rogue charac-
ters, worn-down serifs and punctuation – not all of which were overcome

to my satisfaction. Kerning was also a challenge, and some letters seemed to have been poorly aligned on their bodies.

The sheets were editioned using Van Son inks on a Vandercook 219 proofing press by myself and Susan Baxter between September and December 2000. As most sheets required two colours, each sheet went through the press at least four times. We had a great deal of difficulty maintaining a consistent ink density across such large sheets, especially when printing in cold weather. An original woodblock was engraved for the frontispiece by Wesley W. Bates of West Meadow Press, Clifford, Ontario, and was printed from the block.

The original edition offered two bindings. The paperback edition was hand sewn and bound in a paper cover by Susan Baxter. The leather-bound edition was hand sewn and bound by Ruth Legge. Each book was numbered and stamped with the Gaspereau Press seal to ensure its authenticity.

THIS NEW EDITION of Clarke's *Execution Poems* contains a faithful digital resetting of the text found in the letterpress edition. Typeset in a digital version of Bembo using Adobe InDesign, the text of the book was printed offset on Mohawk Superfine paper and bound at Gaspereau Press. The text is identical to the original, except in the few instances where the shift to the digital realm allowed us to correct design difficulties presented by lead type.

ANDREW STEEVES

GASPEREAU PRESS

EXECUTION POEMS

NEGATION

    Le nègre negated, meagre, *c'est moi*:
A whiskey-coloured provincial, uncouth
Mouth spitting lies, vomit-lyrics, musty,
Masticated scripture. Her Majesty's
Nasty, Nofaskoshan Negro, I mean
To go out shining instead of tarnished,
To take apart poetry like a heart.
    My black face must preface murder for you.

GEORGE & RUE: PURE, VIRTUOUS KILLERS

They were hanged back-to-back in York County Gaol.

They were rough dreamers, raw believers, set out like killers.

They sprouted in Newport Station, Hants County, Nova Scotia,
in 1925 and 1926.

They smacked a white taxi driver, Silver, with a hammer, to lift his silver.

They bopped Silver and hit backwoods New Brunswick in his black cab.

They slew him in the first hour of January 8, 1949, A.D.

They were clear Negro, and semi-Micmac.

They tooled all night between Fredericton and Saint John with Silver
coiled – a void noose – in the trunk.

They had face-to-face trials in May 1949 and backed each other's guilt.

George Albert Hamilton confessed – to theft – and mated the Sally Anne.

Rufus James Hamilton polished his refined, mint, silver-bright English.

They were dandled from a gallows in the third hour of July 27, 1949, A.D.

They were my cousins, dead a decade before I was born.

My bastard phantasms, my dastard fictions.

BALLAD OF A HANGED MAN

Geo: Their drinks to my drinks feels different.
I'll stomach a stammering teaspoon full,
but Roach laps up half the half bottle.
He slups glass for glass with the best.

I sidled in, easy, the taxi with a hammer,
harsh, in my pocket. See, as a wed man,
I don't care if I wear uglified overalls.
But I ain't going to hear my child starve.

I had the intention to ruck some money.
In my own heart, I had that, to rape money,
because I was fucked, in my own heart.
I took scared, shaking inside of me.

I knows Fredericton reporters can prove
zoot-suit vines style not my viciousness.
I was shaking all that evening, my mind,
shaking. But my child was hungered.

Have you ever gone in your life, going
two days without eating, and whenever
you get money, you're gonna eat and eat
regardless of all the bastards in Fredericton

was bust in the head, skull jimmied open?
This is what I'm sermonizing in English:
homemade brew, dug up fresh, tastes like
molasses. We had some. Some good.

Logic does not break down these things, sir.
If I hadn't dropped the hammer, laughing,
Silver would be laughing now. Laughing. Silver
moon and snow dropped on the ground.

Two pieces of bone driven two inches
deep in his brain. What's deeper still?
The bones of the skull were bashed
into the brain. Blood railed out.

I was so mixed up, my mind bent crooked.
Silver's neck, face, and hand bleached cold.
Inside the sedan 19-black-49 sobbing Ford.
Outside, snow and ice smelling red-stained.

I ain't dressed this story up. I am enough
disgraced. I swear to the truths I know.
I wanted to uphold my wife and child.
Hang me and I'll not hold them again.

Rue: Hot pepper of mothers bullwhipped till blood
lava'd down their backs and leapt off their heels
was one-hundred-proof, fire taste of slavery
Pops spooned us raw charring first-hand.

Geo: His whip gashed, splashing into flesh –
what it was made for. The twang
of his whip walloped our shook heads
like a hammer of acid.

Rue: With a swoosh of blood
down the back, the hips, the ass, it shot.
Red sizzled, blazing, off our bodies.
So hot, we felt chills.

Geo: Lash hit us like a whoosh of rain.
Tall screams reared out of Three Mile Plains.
Pops planted two twisted, crooked canes.
See: they flowered into two crooked oaks.

Rue: His fist's width was as long as a horse's cock.
His Decembral love iced over our hearts.

Geo: Pops beat Ma with belts, branches, bottles.
Anything left-handed. Anything at all.
He'd buck Ma onto the bed, buckle his hips to hers.
Slap her across her breasts, blacken them.

Rue: Her terrorized-and tear-shaped breasts.

He thought her being Mulatto
Was mutilation.

(I miss peanut butter cookies, her sewing machine, the grey gloves
she let me present to a schoolgirl, her preacher-lover-dad's second-
hand Shakespeare and tattered scripture she taught me to read, her
confusingly cream-coloured breasts stupefying dazzling under the
threadbare black disintegrating nightshirt she wore to spoonfeed me
oatmeal.)

Geo: Pops smashed Ma like she was Joe Louis.
Stuck a razor to her throat. Struck her down,
pelted soft flesh with fists and bricks.

Rue: I swung a two-by-four and bust Pop's face open.
Kicked the iron bone that was his skull:
Bleeding was so bad I knelt by the stove like I was praying.
I wanted to be God. I wanted him dead.

Geo: Ma fainted scrubbin some white house's blackened crap-box.
She got a heart stoppage and drooped, *kaput.*

Rue: Years, our only real emotion was hunger.
Our thin bellies had to take rain for bread.

CHILD HOOD II

Rue: I craved blue shoes, a yellow suit, and a green shirt —
and jackets sewn from the torn-off, leather covers of books.
I wanted to don jackets emblazoned with *Eugene Onegin,*
Claudine at School, Sonnets from the Portuguese, The Three Musketeers —
all the works of Pushkin, Colette, E. B. Browning, and Alexandre Dumas —
all those secretly Negro authors.

Instead, I witnessed all this:

A boy's right arm stuck to a desk with scissors; a father knifed in the gut
while shaking hands with a buddy; two Christians splashed with gasoline
and set ablaze in a church; a harlot garrotted in her bath; a bootlegger
shot through the eye in a liquor store; a banker brained in a vault; two
artists thrown into the Gaspereau River with their hands tied behind
their backs; a pimp machine-gunned to bits outside a school; a divine
getting his throat slit; a poet axed in the back of the neck; a Tory buried
alive in cement; two diabetics fed cyanide secreted in chocolates; a lawyer
decapitated in his office.

Everywhere I saw a Crimea of crime, calamities of houses rigged from
tarpaper and rape, windows blinded with newsprint or burlap sacks. I
could only start the stove with sparks and fear, watch yellow terror eating
yesterday's bad news.

A poor-quality poet crafting hoodlum testimony,
my watery storytelling's cut with the dark rum of curses.

This is how history darkens against its medium.

I got hallelujah watermelons! – virginal pears! – virtuous corn!
Munit haec et altera vincit!
Luscious, fat-ass watermelons! – plump pears! – big-butt corn!
Le gusta este jardin?
Come-and-get-it cucumbers – hot-to-trot, lust-fresh cucumbers!
Voulez-vous coucher avec moi?
Watermelons! – Go-to-church-and-get-redeemed watermelons!
O peccatore, in verità!
Good God cucumbers! – righteous pears! – golden Baptist corn!
Die Reue ist doch nur ein leuchter Kauf!
I got sluttish watermelons! – sinful cucumbers! – jail-bait pears! –
Planted by Big-Mouth Chaucer and picked by Evil Shakespeare!

IDENTITY I

Rue: My colour is guttural.
I was born in lachrymose air.

My face makes a mess of light:
It's like a black splinter lancing snow.

I'm negative, but positive with a knife.
My instinct? Is to damage someone.

My words collide with walls of fists,
Collapse, my teeth clacking like typewriters.

The encyclopedias encourage rape;
Murder lunges – sable genie – out the radio.

So what? So what? So what? So?
Am I the only nigger in this province with a pistol?

What I am
Cannot be dreamt

By anyone
Imperfect as you.

Geo: Say, Jesus, dapper lady-killer Jesus,
with your snazzy, brash, burnt sienna skin,
your crispy hair like black fire – or a sun, or a halo,
whatcha doin cruisin Three Mile Plains?
    Mary be late at the smoky synagogue
of the tavern, with loud Philistines and poets,
and our ugly whoremasters charge too much.
(Their silver's dirty; their bootleg's deadly.)
    So, whatcha doin, Christ, loungin
in Nova Scotia, with seaweed at your feet,
and April rain, rain, rain, in your eyes?
(Is it because Three Mile Plains
still remains
when all is said and done –
even for the Son of the Sun?)

IDENTITY II

Rue: I remember my mother telling me how to fuck.

This news is followed by photograph-like images, such as films of
myself taking sex, the sound of jails crying, images of Ma stripped in
a shack, and x-rays of my skull, retinas, and mug-shots of my pelvis,
and so on.

Dreams include:

Hatchets of sunlight; a horse's black ass; a decayed dreamer in a cell of
dung; Ma in an attitude of licking my bum; grotesque, gaudy insects;
disgusting infants with snakes' heads; me inside a drum hammered
shut, cringing; vomiting; statues with eyeholes bandaged over; reptiles'
puncturing fangs; plush cockroaches crawling and crawling into and
out of my mouth; red stench of ass blood; a priest being shat on by a
dog; a vague idea of flaps of flesh from incisions made during sodomy.
I hear comparisons of me to a pig, a monkey, a cow. I am alone much.
The burden of bitch-birthed bastardy.

I got out of Dorchester Pen so I could crush violets and butterflies.
My destiny was always murder and to be murdered.

Ain't we such stuff as humus is made of?

Let me drink black rum – ambidextrously.

Geo: Down Ben Jackson Road, you walk the apple-blossom miles of
that old Coloured US Civil War veteran who'd drifted to Nova Scotia
and ploughed near Hantsport. Me and Rufus liked goin there, not
to Eaton's, but to Yeaton's, where they conjure up jaw-bustin candy
and things with sweet, creamy middles. You'd pass the front and smell
chocolate — so strong it was like breathin liquor. Round the back,
you'd sniff alcoholic formaldehyde. Cause Yeaton carves out caskets
— along with candies — at their two-in-one factory. Sometimes,
Yeaton gets formaldehyde confused with the chocolates, or else the
coffins come out with chocolate smutched in the pine or mahogany.
Or, they'd be sweatin on a body in a house, cleanin, embalmin, and
roaches'd scurry over the stiff's legs, then fall drunk on embalmin
fluid, and end up inside the final suit or dress — or in a cigar box
of chocolates. If you eat enough Yeaton chocolates, you die self-
embalmed, all set for burial in a Yeaton casket.

At Cato Pitts's funeral, people spied smoke seepin out his Yeaton
coffin. When Poet States pried up the lid, huge, hateful flames hurled
from Cato's chest and chopped Poet's face and neck, splitting black
skin to bone.

Steps shear from beefy, rancid houses, T-bone into sidewalks.
Or: ramshackle stairs screw into air, then accordion into heaps
of brick-broken bottles, trash, jalopy remains. Rubble
architects the North End, some left over dying
from '17's Explosion, when seamstresses got mashed
by heavy machines crashing through floor after floor,
and schoolkids' eyes shot out, gaudy with glass.
A Canaan of syphilis: Halifax.

On Gottingen St. – sty of sailors' uncivic vices –
Indigo Sampson, pop-eyed drunkard,
violet scar raping his Billy-Eckstine-but-darker face,
remembers wharf rats be so very bad: Like
white gentry promenading in elongated mansions
while black folk pray in taut shacks. This day's not the one –
he's toxic, shabby, cross-eyed, and tizicky –
for two white small boys to accost him, zestfully,
as "n-i-g-g-e-r": He's staggering from killing rats.
His ex-boxer fists – used to hauling junk – elevate an axe.
"Let this blade spit! Let your bloods stink!"

Those two boys disintegrated under his blows,
slicking them with red awfulness. Sampson holds
two blond heads aloft like hauled-up weeds.
He flings two fair splintered bodies into the gutter.
His eyes have fallen; nobody looks at him:
Doors have always been flung in his face, in his face.

His crimson terrors could have garnished the Somme.
Guts dangled crazily from fence posts.
A child's heart was hashed up by rats' pitiless teeth.

[23]

They put Sampson in what he called the *penatenrinary* –
the petty tyranny.
Gallant, pallid guards played at shooting him.
One morning he was sitting with the Bible
and his head popped open;
his black scalp puffed up fatally scarlet.

Rue: When Witnesses sat before Bibles open like plates
And spat sour sermons of interposition and nullification,
While burr-orchards vomited bushels of thorns, and leaves
Rattled like uprooted skull-teeth across rough highways,
And stars ejected brutal, serrated, heart-shredding light,
And dark brothers lied down, quiet, in government graves,
Their white skulls jabbering amid farmer's dead flowers –
The junked geraniums and broken truths of car engines,
And *History* snapped its whip and bankrupted scholars,
School was violent improvement. I opened Shakespeare
And discovered a scarepriest, shaking in violent winds,
Some hallowed, heartless man, his brain boiling blood,
Aaron, seething, demanding, "Is black so base a hue?"
And shouting, "Coal-black refutes and foils any other hue
In that it scorns to bear another hue." O! Listen at that!
I listen, flummoxed, for language cometh volatile,
Each line burning, and unslaked *Vengeance* reddens rivers.
I see that, notwithstanding hosts of buds, the sultry cumuli
Of petals, greatening like the pluvial light in Turner's great
Paintings, the wind hovers – like a death sentence – over
Fields, chilling us with mortality recalcitrant. (Hear now
The worm-sighing waves.) *Sit fas aut nefas*, I am become
Aaron, desiring poisoned lilies and burning, staggered air,
A King James God, spitting fire, brimstone, leprosy, cancers,
Dreaming of tearing down stars and letting grass incinerate
Pale citizens' prized bones. What should they mean to me?
A plough rots, returns to ore; weeds snatch it back to earth;
The stones of the sanctuaries pour out onto every street.
Like drastic Aaron's heir, Nat Turner, I's natural homicidal:
My pages blaze, my lines pall, crying fratricidal damnation.

Geo: We would stink of dying horse and worse —
Sometimes of whores, and get off a horse
And go into whores, and come out worse
Than when we'd gone in: our throats gone hoarse
And our dicks itching hot — as in wars
Where mustard gas rotted flesh — and worse,
And men snuck under every dead horse.

Rue: In Montreal, bus route signs sometimes read "Hors Service."
Anglo bettors wager these trams ferry Blue Bonnet racehorses.
Georgie's worse, dreamin they provide "Whores Service."

Geo: Conversation-piece pussy.

Rue: My good sexistentialism read as a telegram:

At Shushawanna (India) States. — A black-haired beauty. — An
unquenchable bed-fiend. — Tongues and lips. — Hesitation and
consummation. — Is she lewd? Yep. — A ruptured virginity. — French
kisses and English leave. — Da capo. — The Rufus Hamilton train
comes in. — Neophyte harlots and jazz pros. — Champagne and seed.
— Rhumah's face, figure, and colour. — Her sliggery sex. — Aunt
Shushawanna and her niece Rhumah. — Two tartaned tarts. — Indigo
flesh and sable hair. — Shushawanna in bed, simple and indecent.—
Rhumah in the bathroom, filthy and rare.

Their fingers ignited, one-by-one, every bone in my spine.

I remember them for their savings.

GEORGIE'S HIT

Geo: Blondola is good, and her body lovely;
and she is lovely, and her body good.

Her skin be tangerine, dry like white wine;
her hair be deliberately blonde.
But I lick the Sodom of her lips,
lap the Gomorrah of her snatch.

Lovin her's like claspin wasps to my chest –
or the viper of her kisses.
Mine are rats' paws raspin her lips.

I want nothin more but
to go laughin into her blue house,
to stroll through milkweed, daisy, and thistle to a river,

to savour the thrash of fire in her gush,
that hairline fracture twixt her thighs.

HARD NAILS

Geo: Hard nails split my frail bones;
Hard nails gouge my tomb from stone.
Hard nails pierce my feet and hands,
Tack me down so I can't stand.

Hard nails scratch my frail skin;
Hard nails fasten us chin to chin.
Hard nails I want, hard nails I lack –
Her fingernails ploughin my back.

Drench me down with rum and Coca-Cola.
The gal I kiss be a pretty pretty colour.
I ain't got a dollar, but I ain't got no dolour.
Drench me down with rum and Coca-Cola.

DUET

India: Yesterday, I traipsed through an apple orchard
and bit flesh elegantly named "Rosie de Cliej"—
lovely, small, and sweet. So wonderfully healing,
strolling with baskets of apples, a paring knife
in one hand, sharing slices with strangers . . .
I glimpsed a different side of Eve, of Eden.

Rue: I treasure the pleasure of your hands on my back,
your face stirring the heavens to a broth of stars.
Let me kiss your plum lips under plum blossoms,
show you the river cocking through this valley.

India: Wish you were here to taste my "Rosie," "Gala," and "Luck."
I miss the cool ceramic smoothness of your shoulder.
I miss the scent of apple blossoms in the field
and the scent of apple blossoms in our hair —
especially me confusing the two:
The delicate flesh smell of apple blossoms — or whose flesh?

Rue: You move soft — too soft to resist — against resistance.
Look! Your April perfume is still locked, rose madder, in my shirt.

India: Let the moon fall, full throttle, into seas,
lightning, scrunched up, quake into windows.
August wafts a cathedral over us.

Rue: Open your gold mine — suave dark shaft
cream wet with jewelled love — beneath me,
so I'll mine and mine, staking fierce claim,
your kisses puttering rapturous about my face.

India: Why should our talk be like two birds in separate cages?

RUE'S BLUES

I

We fell in love, then fell out –
By two – or one by one.
And all the Latin in a church
Can't union ex-lovers again.

II

Now I'll forego all luxury,
For love drafts no difference:
Jettison love in dark odysseys
From innocence to innocence.

III

Now when I drink black liquor,
It's only memory
Of a bed so warm like sugar,
Her hands stirrin me.

IV

I'll get to the lumber woods
To cut me some pine –
And find me sweeter honey
Lovers can imagine.

SPREE

Rue: .45s smashing into The Palette Restaurant, we corral screaming
swine in a radio-shrieking and ammonia-reeking right-angle, vicious;
smell white money stench on a bitch plus her viscous pimp.

(Hum of money prepared in banks succumbs
to hubbub of coins now brained in the till.)

Gun swats *thap!* up gainst his greasy skull and he tanks –
and she drops slinkily after him, like silk excrement, and I kick
his wallet out his ass pocket, *wallop!* getting farts –
vodka snorting from bad bowels,
while his dame screeches, and Georgie, giggling,
rips her pearls off her craning neck
and the little white balls bullet everywhere.

Bleeding in Nova Scotia is just like drinking.

Rue: Fredericton – fucking – New Brunswick.
A decade of Depression, then the Hitler War.

Carrying my bleak, nasty face out of Nova Scotia,
alarmed, out of Nova Scotia, alarmed,

drift into Fredtown like so much blackstorm sky –
squinting at frigid, ivory, strait-laced streets

speckled by dung of Orange politicians' grins.
(Spy ingots of shit oranging the snow.)

Fredtown was put up by Cadians, Coloureds,
and hammers. Laws and lumber get made here.

Bliss Carman got made here. Why should I put up with
this hard-drinking, hard-whoring, hardscrabble town?

I want to muck up their little white paradise here.
I want to swat their faces til I'm comfortable in my gut.

I want to give em all headaches and nausea:
I'll play *fortissimo* Ellington, blacken icy whiteness.

I'll draw blood the way Picasso draws nudes –
voluptuously.

Geo: If the job is to get money,
a hammer'll do the job.

Rue: It'll effect a cash transfusion,
Georgie, like surgery.

Geo: Nail some wood – or nail a skull.
Rue, we gotta carpenter rascally.

Rue: We'll only fleece Silver of his gold and silver,
not flay his self – fiascoly.

Geo: Then I'll go fetch a hammer.

Rue: But I will use the hammer.
Outlaw deeds carry rough threats of vengeance –
sour honey rotting in the mind,
the small dark box of bitterness.

Geo: I'm gettin the hammer.

(George exits.)

Rue: In a painting, a man takes his head off and blood spurts up.
Beside a gallows.

In life, a man feels his leaden Zeppelin head fizzle onto his chest –
while silvery oxygen spills, deflating his pockets.

THE KILLING

Rue: I ingratiated the grinning hammer
with Silver's not friendless, not unfriendly skull.
Behind him like a piece of storm, I unleashed a frozen glinting –
a lethal gash of lightning.
His soul leaked from him in a Red Sea, a Dead Sea,
churning his clothes to lava.

Geo: No, it didn't look like real blood,
but something more like coal, that inched from his mouth.

Rue: It was a cold hit in the head. A hurt unmassageable.
Car seat left stinking of gas and metal and blood.
And reddening violently.
A rhymeless poetry scrawled his obituary.

Geo: It was comin on us for awhile, this here misery.
We'd all split a beer before iron split Silver's skull.
Silver's muscles still soft and tender. That liquor killed him.
The blood like shadow on his face, his caved-in face.
Smell of his blood over everything.

Rue: Iron smell of the hammer mingled with iron smell of blood
and chrome smell of snow and moonlight.

Geo: He had two hundred dollars on him; bootleg in him.
We had a hammer on us, a spoonful of cold beer in us.

The taxi-driver lies red in the alabaster snow.
His skeleton has taken sick and must be placed in the ground.

This murder is 100 per cent dirt of our hands.

Rue: Twitchy, my hand was twitchy, inside my jacket.
The hammer was gravity: everything else was jumpy.
I wondered if Silver could hear his own blood thundering,
vermilion, in his temples, quickened, twitchy, because of beer;
jumpy molecules infecting his corpuscles, already nervous.

The hammer went in so far that there was no sound –
just the slight mushy squeak of bone.

Silver swooned like the leaden Titanic.
Blood screamed down his *petit-bourgeois* clothes.

Geo: Can we cover up a murder with snow?
With white, frosty roses?

Rue: Here's how I justify my error:
The blow that slew Silver came from two centuries back.
It took that much time and agony to turn a white man's whip
into a black man's hammer.

Geo: No, we needed money,
so you hit the So-and-So,
only much too hard.
Now what?

Rue: So what?

Geo: Doc stared gravely, said, "You're going to die."
I glared, spat, "So will you."

. . .

Geo: My speech? Pretty ugly. Those who complain? Uglier.
My English is like fractured China – broken.
I really speak *Coloured*, but with a Three Mile Plains accent.
See, I can't speak Lucasville and my New Road's kinda weak.
Ma English be a desert that don't bloom less watered by rum.

. . .

Geo: Yonder, that horse is fat, its hairs full of sweat.
I love my wife and two childs and I'd hold them yet.

. . .

Geo: This is a good apple country. Right so. I would like to get
on the Dominion Atlantic Railway drivin an engine. If I could go to
Africa, to a Coloured country, or to Haiti, or even to Cuba, I would
go. I would like to get away. On a no-moon night when the only
eyes that got vision are God's. Oh, if I could get away, I would do
away with sickness and not get away with murder. Who can do more
and more and more injustice?

TRIAL II

Rue: This courtroom's a parliament of jackals –
see Hitler faces front dark robes.

Unsullied, though, a wafer of light silvers water;
unspoiled, the wind rattles alders.

    I would like very much to sing –
in a new life, a new world,
some April song –
"A slight dusting of snow,
the indigo dawn hovers –
and we sweeten in our love,"
yes, something like that,
but blood must expunge, sponge up, blood.

We're condemned because death is not condemned.
We're damned because desire is not damned.

Stars are hanging like locusts in the trees.

Birds faction the air.

April collapses snow into flowers.

The river goes cloudy with moon.

MALIGNANT ENGLISH

Crown: I warrant you speak almost perfect English.

Rue: Should I utter pitted and cankered English?
Bad enough your laws are pitted and cankered.

Crown: Admit that, for a Negro, you speak our English well.

Rue: But, your alabaster, marble English isn't mine: I hurl
insolent daggers at it like an assassin assaulting a statue.

Crown: Your Lordship, instruct this witness to speak civilly.

His Lordship: Accused, do your duty, as we must do ours.

Rue: My duty is to make narrative more telling,
Yours is to make malice more malicious.

PROSECUTION

Crown: God-glorifying, Bible-backing people
don't do what you boys did.

Your faces are ochre;
your thought mediocre.

Unanimously
pusillanimous,

you have abolished a father;
you have annihilated a husband.

Starting with the first, majuscule letter, that sturdy "H,"
you have made a gallows of your surname.

Your not earth-stained, not ink-stained,
but, yes, blood-stained, hands
must be legislated into grass.

The Crown demands green slime scum over your black souls.

(The grass already surges, insolent as whips.)

AVOWALS

A is a cracked steeple.
E is a long scream.
I is a gawky guillotine.
O is a silk abyss.
U is a fetus — or crab lice.
Y is a two-pronged gallows.

FAMOUS LAST

Rue: Hanging Gardens of Babylon?
Nope, hanging niggers in Fredericton!
We'll hang like Christ hanged.

Geo: The laws preach Christ, but teach crucifixion.
Folks glance through us like we're albino ghosts.

Rue: Hanging's a lot like drowning:
The condemned pedal in air,
while constriction inundates the throat.

We'll be *disjecta membra* of Loyalist New Brunswick.
We'll furiously spew up air as we fall.
We'll try to eat your faces through our hoods.
We'll plunge our bodies into pools of air,
into coffins snug as our shadows,
the shallow graves of morning news.

Geo: I can't forgive this fierce world. Forgive me.
(Forgive me, my darling wife and my little ones.)

Rue: We will fall into our sentence: silence.

We will watch night shudder as stars fall.

TO VISCOUNT ALEXANDER OF TUNIS,
GOVERNOR-GENERAL OF CANADA

Anonamus
Fredericton N.B.
May 30th 1949

I understand a neggar name Georges Hamilton has ritten to
you fore merci i find as all citizens of Fred dose this was one
of the most brutal, most turrable, murders ever done in the
provence of Nouveau Brunswick and while he claims he did
not kill the man or rather hit the dead man on the head
with a hammer he was pronouned guilty for he was just as
evilish as his bruther Rufus – Rudy – for after burgundy
was sstruck he and his borther dugged the body out the carr
and robed him and then jammed the body in trunk of car
with George keep mashin the murdered man's foot with the
trunk lid (not firming it right) and then Careened to Sant
john NB and skwandered the messed man's money and left
then left the dead carr on a bleak road and was found some
days later he jeorge Hamilton Clamed he need argent to
pay his wife doctor bill as she was in hospital he never
used a Cent of this money fore that purpos but the money
was split between him and his brother Rudy and splashed
on Woman and swallowed in Rum and Eatables he Claims
murcey on account of his wife and children. he did not
show any murrsey on the man killed as he got a wife and
sept children and this citizen was well-thought of and was
earning a pure living fore to keep his family he was not let
any chance to defend him self and never done Ither of this
Convects harm burrgundee was a returned war man who
fought fore his country this George Hamilton and his Rufus
brot her never was out of Canada (or trouble) and I have
been told that George Hamilton was thrown out the Army

with a dishonorable discharge he have a *black* record as a
theif and will not work his brother have done a turm in
dorchuster fore robery and assult he claims he have turned a
Chrisschun now this i do not beleave i am of the faith this
is only a sham to *deseive* the people and cheat justis i tell you
of this Sir out of duty. he is pronouned to be hanged a long
with his Rudy broth er on July 27 – 49. he had a fear trial and
was capabull defend and wee the peepul of Fredericton feel
they must hang fore the bluddy homaside they did

Yours Very Truly
A Citizen of the town of Fredricton NB

Ps. no dout he have put all the blame on his brother Rudy as
he done at his trial they is no different neggars & they both
look a like in this Cryme

VOICE OF THE PEOPLE

Dear Editor:
 Moon is a white plum
 dangled from black, bare branches,
 ripe with August frost.

– *S. Hamilton,*
Newport Station, N.S.

CRIMINAL ERROR

An article published in last week's edition
asserts that Spear Flowers strangled Nicey
Pew in 1948. Flowers has written us to
say he actually murdered Pew in 1947. We
also reported that Flowers killed Pew
"after the pair had shared two bottles of
red wine." However, Flowers insists that
the homicide occurred after they had
shared three jugs of white wine. He also
complains that our mistake implies that he
committed his crime because of
intoxication. Instead, he wishes us to
make it clear that he strangled Pew to
death because she had begun to write
poetry, though he prefers true crime. We
hereby retract our incorrect comments.
But why should we kowtow to a killer?

LITERARY ERROR

In an article on dead poet W. B. Yeats in
last week's *Casket*, we erroneously
attributed to Mr. Yeats the book *Cane*,
which was in fact written by the Negro
American writer Jean Toomer. Yeats is,
however, the author of the best-selling
book *The Autobiography of William Butler
Yeats.* We regret the error.

HAMILTONS HANGED
EARLY THIS MORNING
FOR BURGUNDY MURDER;
*TRAP SPRUNG SHORTLY AFTER 2
A.M. 1,000 CITIZENS TRIED TO SEE
DYING MEN AS THEY SWUNG.*

FREDERICTON – A deuce of Barker's
Point negroes died on the gallows here this
morning.
 They paid the penalty *in extremis.*
 The execution site proved irresistible for
roughly 1,000 curious on-lookers from the
city, nearby farms, and from as far away as
Boston. Every close rooftop, line fence,
window and woodpile was occupied as the
throng, including babes-at-suck and grey
pates, clogged the gaol yard entrance and
vantage points to eye the two doomed
negroes as they were guided from their cells
to the gallows in the barn loft in the York
County Gaol yard.
 Gathering as early as 10 o'clock, the mob
hung with fanatical tenacity until twin
corpses were motored from the gaol yard to
the Roman Catholic and Protestant
cemeteries for burial about an hour after
the two hangings.
 Heralded by the tolling of St. Dunstan's
Church bell, directly across the street from
the gaol, the arrival of Sheriff I. B. Lion and
the pseudonymous hangman "Arthur Ellis"
from Montreal on the stroke of two o'clock
signalled the falling of the final curtain on
the grim sequel to the Tragedy of the
Richibucto Road murder last January.
 Barred from the interior of the gaol and
scene of the double hanging, newsmen
from a vantage point near the two-storey
grey-stone building could see only the
condemned men's shadows as they glided
from the upper corridor and guyed down
the stairs to the side entrance of the Gaol.

[44]

The double hanging was executed according to law.

Finis the Tragedy of "George and Rue."

GEORGE ELLIOTT CLARKE was born in Windsor, Nova Scotia.
He has published four books of poetry, including *Whylah Falls* (1990),
which won the Archibald Lampman Award, and *Beatrice Chancy*
(1999). In 1998, Clarke was awarded the prestigious
Portia White Prize. He is presently lecturing
at the University of Toronto.

AUTHOR'S DISCLAIMER
The crime of this poetry could not have been committed
without the aid of Andrew Steeves, David Odhiambo,
John Fraser, and Anne Compton. However, they bear no
responsibility for its harms. Only the author deserves hanging.

This book was originally hand set in lead type and printed letterpress at Gaspereau Press in a limited edition of 66 books. This trade paperback edition first appeared in February 2001 and was typeset in Adobe Bembo by Andrew Steeves and printed offset at Gaspereau Press on Mohawk Superfine paper. The typeface is based on roman letters cut in Venice by Francesco Griffo in 1495. First issued by Monotype in 1929, Bembo is named for poet and historian Pietro Bembo (1470-1547) whose book, *De Aetna*, is thought to be the first to use Griffo's typeface. The frontispiece is reproduced, slightly reduced in size, from a wood engraving made by Wesley W. Bates for the original letterpress edition.

Print shop photos by Nyla Trimper and George Elliott Clarke. Author photo by Geeta Paray-Clarke. Photo of the hanged man, Josée F. Ama (d.1932), by Victor-Gabriel Brodeur (National Defence Collection, National Archives of Canada).

Gaspereau Press acknowledges the support of the Canada Council for the Arts.

5

CANADIAN CATALOGUING IN PUBLICATION DATA

Clarke, George Elliott, 1960–
Execution poems

Poems
1-894031-35-0 (LIMITED ED., LEATHER)
1-894031-34-2 (LIMITED ED., PBK)
1-894031-48-2 (PBK)
1. Title.
PS8555.L374E94 2001   C811'.54   C2001-900078-2
PR9199.3.C53E94 2001

GASPEREAU PRESS
WOLFVILLE, NOVA SCOTIA